TITANI

The Story About The Unsinkable Ship

BY

Henry Freeman

© 2016 Copyright

Table of Contents

Introduction

The RMS [1] Titanic struck an iceberg on the night of April fourteenth 1912, and sank in the North Atlantic waters in the wee hours of the following morning. She took more than 1,500 souls with her. While this death toll is devastating, it is by no means the greatest at-sea catastrophe in western history. Even besides wartime disasters, the explosion of the Mont-Blanc in Nova Scotia killed almost two thousand in 1917, the 1707 Sicily Naval Disaster killed almost the same number of people, and several other shipwrecks with smaller death tolls were arguably more dramatic. Yet fascination with the Titanic has persisted since she rested on the ocean floor, long before James Cameron's 1997 blockbuster film. Why?

In many ways, the sinking of the Titanic can be seen as the perfect, tragic end to an era of seemingly boundless technological innovation as well as decadent lifestyles built on vast inequalities of wealth. As has been popularly remembered, many people believed that "God himself cannot sink this ship" (although the ship's builders never went so far as to make that claim). People truly believed that the technological innovations surrounding shipbuilding and other industries had made the Titanic invincible. When she did sink, on her maiden voyage, this confidence in human innovation was shaken. Ensuing investigations would search for an explanation that would allow them to reassert their confidence, but in the end they came up empty-handed. Barely two years later, this shaken confidence in human progress would be shattered as Europe and the world plunged into World War I, which saw unprecedented death (the death toll is estimated at seventeen million) and destruction at the hands of new wartime technologies.

Several prominent businessmen — "robber barons" — went down with the ship as well, including John Jacob Astor IV and Benjamin Guggenheim. The years that followed would also see a challenge to their kind of entrenched wealth and power: when World War I ended, labor riots erupted in countries around the world. While labor unrest had been fomenting for decades, the riots of 1919 were especially violent and the fear of communism swept the western world. In addition, a virulent influenza epidemic spread globally in 1918-1919, killing a staggering twenty to forty million people. Perhaps these factors help explain our collective fascination with the Titanic disaster: it occurred at a time that allows it to symbolize the end of an era of wealthy, gallant gentlemen; faith in technological progress; and a sense of optimism about the future. Regardless, the story of the Titanic is an enthralling tale, from its conception, to its demise, to its re-discovery decades later.

[1] *RMS stands for "Royal Mail Ship," which simply means that the ship carried mail for the British government's mail service.*

Chapter One

Conceiving of and Building the Titanic

The Titanic was built by the White Star Line, a British shipping company controlled by the International Mercantile Marine Company. The idea for the ship was broached first in 1907 when the White Star Line faced stiff competition in the passenger ship market. Their main competitors were the German-owned Hamburg America line and the British-owned Cunard line (which merged with the White Star Line in 1934 and now operates Carnival Cruise Line). Cunard had recently launched two new remarkable ships that made trans-Atlantic voyages, the RMS Mauritania and the RMS Lusitania (which also sank in 1915). Both were primarily known for their speed, so J.P. Morgan, the infamous American banker who owned controlling shares in the International Mercantile Marine Company, and J. Bruce Ismay, the head of the White Star Line, decided that they would compete on luxury. They would build ships that were still fast, but were more appealing because their grandeur would outmatch all the competition.

The Titanic was one of three ships built under this plan: the Olympic was the first, Titanic was the second, and Britannic was the third. Britannic also met an untimely end: it hit a mine and sank in 1916 during World War I, while the Olympic remained in service until 1935. The White Star Line operated the ships, but they did not build them: all three ships were built in Belfast, Ireland by the firm Harland and Wolff. This company dispatched its most prominent employees for the construction of the grand ships, especially the Titanic, including their chairman Lord William James Pirrie (largely responsible for decisions regarding the number of lifeboats), his brother-in-law and designer Right Honorable Alexander Carlisle (who would leave the company over a dispute with Pirrie about the number of lifeboats), and Thomas Andrews, a shipbuilder and architect (who was on board for the maiden voyage and died in the sinking). The White Star Line had worked with Harland and Wolff in the past; this time, they gave the company a great amount of leeway in the ships' design and the costs. Harland and Wolff developed plans for the first two ships, for the base amount of three million British pounds. These plans were approved and signed in July 1908. In the end, the Titanic would cost about 7.5 million pounds to construct, a staggering sum of money at the time.

Construction on the Titanic officially began later in 1908. Harland and Wolff actually had to destroy some of their infrastructure and build new slipways in order to construct the massive ships (Olympic and Titanic were largely built at the same time). Also, before the era of government regulations and labor laws, ship construction was very dangerous. Titanic actually claimed her first victims long before April 1912: eight died during construction, and twenty-eight severe injuries were recorded. More than 240 people were hurt in total.

The Titanic was launched in May 1911, when she sailed a short distance to the place where she would be completed (much of the interior outfitted). As with any major disaster in world history, legends surrounding the Titanic abound. One of the earliest is that the ship was cursed because it was not "christened" before it made this first journey. However, the White Star Line did not typically christen its ships at all, and many of them survived many voyages despite this lack of ritual. One fact is true, though: her completion was delayed when Olympic needed unscheduled repairs. While speculation in history is never rock-solid, it is reasonable to think that had the Titanic been launched on schedule, she may not have hit the iceberg.

The Titanic encountered more unfortunate luck during its construction and outfitting phases than just bad timing. Some historians have cited two critical mistakes made in the design stage of the ship that would cost so many lives. The first was, of course, the number of lifeboats. One of the most devastating mistakes made during the sinking was not loading the boats to capacity (which we will discuss in a later chapter), but even if they had, the boats could only have safely held about 1,200 people at the most. That means that at least one thousand souls still would have perished, even if each boat had been filled to capacity (and had the Titanic been full on her only voyage, at least one thousand more would have also died). This was not only a failure on the part of Harland and Wolff or even the White Star Line; the lifeboat capacity actually exceeded government regulations at the time (though the Titanic disaster would prompt these regulations to change). Regardless, there were some people who believed that this ship, and any ship, should carry more lifeboats – though they were ignored. In addition, the watertight doors were a much-boasted safety feature, which was one of the reasons that the ship (and others like it at the time) was thought to be "unsinkable." However, the Titanic was actually not equipped with the most up-to-date technology in this respect. Water was able to breach these doors and flood the entire ship. Had the technology to prevent this from happening been employed (some Cunard ships had installed it), it is within the realm of possibility that the ship could have been saved, and more likely that the Carpathia would have reached the Titanic in time to save all of her passengers.

As with the launch of any new ship, the Titanic underwent trials at sea before taking on passengers for her trans-Atlantic maiden voyage. These took place only about a week before she was scheduled to begin this journey. These kinds of tests were rather rudimentary: they made sure that the ship's equipment functioned correctly and could perform basic and some unexpected tasks. All in all, the trials lasted only one day. Afterward, the Titanic set out to sea from Belfast, Ireland, to Southampton, England, located on the south-central part of the island on the English Channel. It would be in Southampton that the ship would take on the first portion (and the majority) of its ill-fated crew and passengers.

Chapter Two

"The Ship of Dreams"

Harland and Wolff, as well as all who collaborated on the construction of the Titanic, spared no expense in making sure that it was the most luxurious vessel on the water, and they certainly earned the nickname "the ship of dreams." Once complete, she was not only massive, but incredibly impressive and luxurious. The Titanic boasted more than 800 staterooms and eleven decks outfitted in opulent style and comfort. Even third class accommodations surpassed the competition.

Obviously, the first class accommodations were the most luxurious. Being aboard the Titanic in first class would be comparable to staying in a grand, five-star hotel today. There was a lot to occupy first class passengers' time: they could play squash on the squash courts, swim in the pool, exercise in the gym, or take a steam in the Turkish Baths (similar to today's saunas). While gender segregation was typically no longer the rule in turn-of-the-century high society, the ship still respected prevailing social norms by having areas that were intended for use by either women or men. The smoking room was designed primarily for gentlemen. A dark room with much mahogany in the decor, it also featured a bar. In contrast, the reading and writing room was intended to be a female space. It was light, airy and warm: white walls, expansive windows to allow deck and sea views, and a large fireplace were its main features. Meanwhile, the first class lounge was meant for members of both sexes to mingle. It was a multi-purpose room, and passengers played cards and games, socialized, read books, and wrote letters and postcards. It was a gathering place, and a good room in which to spend your time during the day if you wished to mingle with some of the other elite guests.

In addition to these entertainment areas, Titanic passengers dined in absolute elegance, which was typical for members of the upper class of the day whether at sea or on land. The main dining room was where dinner was served each night. The dining room was massive; it was the largest on any ship in the world, and could seat more than five hundreds diners. Dinner was probably the most important social point of the day; men wore suits or tuxedos and women sometimes spent hours dressing in gowns and doing their hair. Dinner was several courses (the last dinner on the Titanic was ten courses), with time in between to digest, and usually lasted several hours. All in attendance were expected to converse intelligently, but with the proscribed decorum of the day. Some examples of the food served at dinner include oysters, lamb with mint sauce, poached salmon with mousseline sauce, and roasted sirloin with mushroom demi. Even breakfast was an elaborate affair. Some breakfast dishes included baked apples, Findon haddock, and various exotic marmalades. In addition to the main dining room, the ship also featured a French-style restaurant. The food here was not included in passenger fare, so anything eaten here cost extra. It was an elaborately decorated room meant to evoke the French style of Louis XIV, and many guests visited simply to see and be seen, and to sample the rich cuisine.

Additionally, the Titanic featured other common space for first class. Certainly, the most iconic was the Grand Staircase, and that it was: grand. It was about 6 stories from the lower level up to the glass enclosure above (which shattered during the sinking). The glass let in fabulous light that shone off the wide, rich wood steps. It was ornately adorned; in addition to beautiful wrought-iron and wood banisters and railings, it featured a wood-carved clock and wooden cherub light fixture at the foot. First class passengers marveled at its beauty, and its relatively central location meant that it became a fixture of their time on the ship. Most guests would pass it on their way to dinner, since there was a large reception room directly behind it where guests often congregated before sitting down for that elaborate meal.

Then of course there were the first class staterooms themselves. Just as in a five-star hotel, all the rooms were nice, but some were fancier (and more expensive) than others. For the twelve most opulent staterooms, a design firm used by Dutch royalty was called in: H.P. Mutters & Zoon. These and the other suites featured bedrooms, private bathrooms, dressing rooms, and parlors. All were lavishly outfitted in a variety of design styles, including those of various French kings. Other, simpler rooms were still comfortable, and somewhat resembled a hotel room of today: bed, table, fireplace, chaise or lounge, writing desk, and sink.

These simpler rooms were sometimes occupied by the staff of wealthier first class passengers, their personal stewards without whom they could (or would) not travel. They also resembled a standard room in second class. There were a few single rooms in second class with single beds, but most rooms included bunk beds to accommodate families. They, too, featured a sitting area and sink, though second class passengers shared communal bathrooms. The White Star Line recognized that their first class accommodations would be out of reach for most people, but they also understood that many members of the middle-class still wanted to travel in style, especially compared to the more basic third class accommodations. Thus, the Titanic's second class was also luxuriously outfitted. Several common areas, similar to the ones in first class, were available to second class passengers. Second class also featured a smoking room and a library: like the smoking room and reading and writing room in first class, these were gendered spaces. Women often congregated in the library while men spent their free time in the smoking room, especially after dinner. Particularly compared to other similar spaces in second class on other ships, these were especially beautiful. Deep woods like mahogany and thick, elegant fabrics were used in the furniture and design. There was also an opulent dining room that could easily accommodate all the guests booked in second class at one time, even if all the rooms were full. Breakfast foods included fried eggs and potatoes, grilled sausage and ham, and fresh fruit; for lunch, roast mutton and roast beef, pea soup, and apple tart were served; and at dinner, passengers were offered multiple courses (though not as many as first class) which included dishes like roast turkey with cranberry sauce, curried chicken and rice, ice cream, and cheese and biscuits.

Stark differences obviously marked third class, which was primarily occupied by laborers and immigrants. However, third class on the Titanic was superior to third class on many contemporary ships. Popular portrayals of third class on board the Titanic are rather harsh; certainly, they were less luxurious than second class, but the White Star Line did go above and beyond to provide for these passengers. They wanted all souls on board to have a one-of-a-kind experience. As in first and second classes, third class was outfitted with several communal areas. They, too, had a smoking room. They also had a common room, where passengers could gather during the day and evening to enjoy activities similar to second and even first class: playing cards and games, socializing, meeting new people, reading, et cetera. Their dining room was also very large: it extended from starboard to port, and about one hundred feet lengthwise. For breakfast, third class passengers could have oatmeal, ham and eggs, or fresh bread. For dinner, roast beef, sweet corn, rice soup, and potatoes were available, among other items. Interestingly, the third class menus carried a message for passengers: it directed them to report any poor treatment on the part of staff immediately, and contained instructions for who to report to and how to identify the offender. Clearly, the White Star Line cared that these passengers had a pleasant experience, as well.

Third class staterooms afforded much less privacy than second class. There were eighty-four rooms with two beds, but these were more expensive than the larger cabins, which housed either four or six passengers. Families could rent these rooms together, but unless they took the whole room, staterooms were designated either male or female, so very often third class passengers traveled with strangers. Still, these were smaller rooms than seen on other ships at the time, and each room was equipped with a sink. There were also large, communal bathrooms on board, and reports suggest that they were kept impeccably clean, a remarkable feat in consideration of the fact that over a thousand people used them every day.

Passengers of all classes could enjoy the outdoors, though in segregated areas. First class occupied the airiest, most open upper decks, with comfortable deck chairs in which to lounge. Outdoor areas in second class were less opulent, and third class featured mostly benches. Yet despite the cold air, the Titanic and her passengers enjoyed mostly sunny, clear weather, so it is easy to assume that many passengers took advantage of the sea views on their voyage.

While first class passengers were allowed to use second and third class amenities, and second class was allowed to use third class amenities, there was very little mixing of the classes aboard the ship. Most passengers stayed among their "own kind." As society in general had become more stratified in many ways (for example, cities had distinct slums and wealthy areas), the construction and the social world of the Titanic reflected these patterns, for better or for worse. Locked doors meant to deny passengers access to higher-class facilities would actually end up delaying access to lifeboats. Even more segregated were the members of the crew. Under no circumstances did the ship's designers want the crew mingling with the passengers, so their sleeping and eating areas and even the staircases they typically used to get to and from meals and work were "behind the scenes." They were more modest than third class, and more communal, but the White Star Line nonetheless wanted their staff well-rested and fed.

Chapter Three

Setting Sail

After she passed her sea trials and the outfitting was complete, the Titanic scheduled to begin her maiden voyage on Wednesday, April 10, 1912. While most other White Star Line vessels (as well as vessels belonging to their main competitor, Cunard) sailed out of Liverpool, England, and although the Titanic was registered in Liverpool, she was to set sail out of Southampton instead. Southampton offered a couple of advantages, including proximity to both London and France. Titanic picked up passengers first in Southampton on the morning of April 10, setting sail about noon. The majority of passengers and crew embarked here. After the crew, third class passengers boarded, for a few of reasons: first, there were more of them, which meant it would take the longest to get them on board. Second, they had to undergo a medical inspection which, while brief, took additional time since it had to be repeated hundreds of times. And, of course, class considerations come into play here as well: second and then first class passengers could take their time getting to the dock, and would not have to worry about being there among too many third class passengers.

The first day was not smooth sailing; the Titanic narrowly averted disaster not once, but twice, as it left Southampton. Before steaming out, a fire was discovered in the coal room. It was mostly put out, and when the chief engineer inspected the damage with the captain, both men decided that it was not drastic enough to delay departure. Then, as the massive ship left the port, her size caused unexpected wake and sea disturbance that snapped cords holding the S.S. City of New York in place, and the Titanic nearly had a collision with the smaller vessel. Superstitious history buffs read much into this incident: first, it has been interpreted as a bad omen for the voyage generally. Secondly, the ship was named for the very city to which the Titanic was bound. And third, had the collision actually occurred, the damage could have been severe enough to delay sailing and thus the disaster may have been averted. But despite these hiccups, the Titanic set out.

Titanic did not steam out into the Atlantic after leaving Southampton. Rather, she headed across the English Channel to Cherbourg, in northern France, where about three hundred more passengers embarked. By eight o'clock, as many passengers were enjoying their first dinner on board the ship, she headed toward Queenstown, on Ireland's southern coast. They arrived in Queenstown (now Cobh) around 11:30 am the next day, and picked up about 120 more passengers, before finally heading out to sea at 1:30 pm. There were several very fortunate souls in both Cherbourg and Queenstown — these were the people who disembarked. Over thirty individuals went ashore in these two cities. They may have been disappointed to leave such a magnificent vessel at the time, but doubtless they counted their blessings on the morning of April 15. Among them was a photographer, Francis Browne (a Jesuit priest), and it is thanks to him (and the fact that he departed the ship) that we have photographs of any portion of the maiden voyage. He took dozens of images, including one of men using the gymnasium, several of people walking, watching, or playing outside on the decks (including children), the radio room, the reading room, the dining room, and the menu planned for the day of the sinking.

Events proceeded normally on that first day at sea. The Titanic followed a well-traveled route across the Atlantic toward her destination, New York City. As has been well-remembered, she made tremendous speed over the few days that she sailed. While many suspicions abounded in the immediate aftermath and persist today that the captain was under pressure to set a record in the time it took to reach New York, these have actually not been substantiated and are almost certainly false. In addition, the Titanic's speed probably had little to do with her sinking: it was not unusual for large ships to travel at full speed or close to it, even amid warnings of icebergs. What is more, large ships had survived collisions with icebergs in the recent past and completed their journeys.

On Thursday and Friday, April eleventh and twelfth, the weather remained somewhat mild and improved as the Titanic moved further into the Atlantic. Temperatures were warm enough for passengers to spend time outdoors, winds were relatively calm, and skies clear. On Saturday the thirteenth, however, temperatures turned colder. While the sea would remain calm and the skies clear throughout the day of the fourteenth, temperatures continued to plunge. This colder night air of the 14th-15th made the sinking more unbearable, though it probably did not contribute much to the death toll: of those who did not drown or die from other causes (being crushed by falling machinery, for example), those that died from cold did so due to the water temperatures, which would not have been much warmer in such deep seas that time of year even if the weather had improved a few degrees. The only possible impact that the cold air may have had was in the loading of the lifeboats early on in the evening: it took some time for the passengers to realize that the sinking was a real emergency. Resistance among first class women to leave the warmth and presumed safety of the ship, not to mention resistance on the part of their husbands, may have contributed to the fact that most of the lifeboats were not filled to capacity.

Chapter Four

The Passengers

Perhaps thanks in large part to James Cameron's film Titanic, many people are familiar with the disparities between first and third class accommodations and passengers aboard the vessel. Of the 2,223 people who made the voyage, more than three hundred first class passengers were on board, compared to about 700 in third class. Second class was largely composed of middle class workers, including intellectuals, religious figures, lawyers, mid-level businessmen, et cetera. There was just under three hundred second class passengers. In addition, many if not most first class passengers also brought along their servants, and the entire crew of the Titanic made up the rest of the total, ranging in skill level from captain to coal shoveler.

By happy circumstance, the Titanic was not fully booked on its maiden voyage. The United Kingdom was experiencing a coal strike in the months leading up to the sailing, and this turbulence caused many potential passengers to postpone their journeys, much like an airline worker strike now might cause people to postpone air travel when possible. Coal powered the Titanic and other steamships at the time, and the strike had been disrupting sea travel.

The first class passengers are certainly the best-remembered, and for good reason: among them were some of the most illustrious names of the day. The Titanic's maiden voyage was a very big deal, and a massive public relations campaign had been undertaken to make sure that the best and richest of high society were on board. In fact, even the most basic first class accommodations would today cost more than 2,000 British pounds.

The wealthiest passenger was, without a doubt, John Jacob Astor IV (the great-grandson of John Jacob Astor, who created America's first trust and also became the new country's first multimillionaire in the early nineteenth century). Astor IV was worth close to one hundred million dollars at the time, a staggering sum in 1912. He was returning from his European honeymoon with his new wife, Margaret. He had scandalized the American elite "blue-bloods" by divorcing his first wife and marrying Margaret, who was only eighteen years old at the time, twenty-nine years his junior. The pair had intended to remain abroad longer in order to let the scandal die down, but Margaret became pregnant during the trip and wanted her baby born in the United States. They thus took advantage of their exalted status to book passage on the famous Titanic's upcoming maiden voyage. Astor IV did not survive the sinking; he perished along with the couple's dog, Kitty, and is remembered as one of the noble wealthy gentlemen who went down with the ship. However, he would have apparently taken a seat in a lifeboat: he asked to be allowed into a lifeboat with his pregnant young wife, and was denied. Margaret, however, did get into one of the boats and survived. She gave birth to a son a few months later, named John Jacob Astor in honor of her late husband. She remarried twice, but also died early at the age of forty-six.

While much of "high society" was at least scandalized by and at most shunned this newlywed couple (one of thirteen honeymooning couples on board), one woman of some notoriety did not: the widow Margaret Tobin Brown actually spent time with the couple while they traveled in France. An American-born child of Irish immigrants, she married James Joseph Brown in 1886 in Colorado. He became wealthy by developing mining technology, and she became well-known in Denver, Colorado, and throughout the United States for her philanthropic efforts. She cared deeply about women's rights, children's welfare, and humanity in general, so it is not surprising that as the Titanic disappeared beneath the icy North Atlantic waters and she heard the cries of survivors, she forced the representatives of the White Star Line at the helm of lifeboat 6 to turn around and look for survivors. While she is best remembered as the "Unsinkable Molly Brown," she did not earn this moniker until after her death in 1932 at age sixty-five. However, she did use the notoriety that she earned in the aftermath of the sinking to draw attention to other human rights causes about which she was deeply concerned.

Another famous American couple on board the Titanic was Isidor and Ida Strauss, who owned Macy's Department Store. Isidor was born in Germany and immigrated to the U.S. as a child. He married Rosalie Ida Blun, also a German immigrant, and the couple had seven children. He and his brother worked their way up within R.H. Macy's store to eventual ownership, and Isidor served a single two-year term in the U.S. House of Representatives from New York State. Yet the Strausses are much better known for their final expressions of love, which are present in almost all representations of the tragic night of April 14-15, 1912. Many are familiar with the cry of "women and children first!" that cost many men their lives. Even though Ida was offered (more than once) a seat on a lifeboat, she refused to leave her husband's side. Equally stubborn, Isidor refused seats offered to him when there were still women and children on board, especially as it became apparent that not everyone would get a seat on a lifeboat. Many survivors reported seeing the couple holding each other shortly before the ship broke in half and sank.

Several members of the British aristocracy were also on board for the ship's maiden voyage, including Sir Cosmo and Lady Lucy Duff Gordon. Cosmo was not only known for his Scottish aristocratic pedigree (he inherited his title), but also for being an Olympic fencing silver medalist in 1906, and for helping to plan the 1908 Olympic Games. Lucy, known during her life as "Madame Lucile", was a much-sought fashion designer; she worked only with the most elite clients, including members of the British Royal Family. Unlike the Strausses and Margaret Brown, though, his legacy was tarnished in the aftermath of the sinking. For one thing, he was a man who boarded a lifeboat early on, seemingly in violation of the order (and law of the sea) to give women and children priority. To compound this faux-pas, there were only twelve people in his lifeboat when the total capacity was forty. If that was not bad enough, he was accused of bribing the crew of the lifeboat not to return to the site of the wreck to pick up survivors after the ship sank. While he was exonerated of these charges (it was accepted that any transfer of moneys was a donation), his reputation never recovered, especially when stories of heroism and gallantry abounded.

Like Margaret Brown, other women were also regarded as heroines of the disaster. The Countess of Rothes, Lucy Noël, is another. She is remembered for helping row her lifeboat to the safety of the Carpathia (the ship that arrived to pick up survivors) when crew and other passengers were either weak, grief-stricken, or in shock. She continued to be a very charitable figure after the sinking of the ship (perhaps the experience was life-changing for her). She became active in the Red Cross, especially during World War I, and lived until 1956, to the age of seventy-seven.

Also traveling in first class were representatives of the White Star Line and Harland and Wolff. Much like Duff Gordon, J. Bruce Ismay, the White Star Line's Managing Director, survived by climbing into a lifeboat, with the result being that his reputation was tarnished for the rest of his life. The ship's designer, Thomas Andrews, died in the sinking. The White Star Line's chairman, Lord Pirrie, was too sick to make the trip despite wanting to do so, and he was not the only person to narrowly miss the disaster: J.P. Morgan, who was integral to planning and financing the ship, missed its maiden voyage, as did Milton S. Hershey, the candy baron.

While the illustrious names of first class passengers did not show up in the other classes, many souls also traveled in second and third class. Many of them lost their lives, lost their loved ones, or were forever changed by the experience. One such individual was William H. Harbeck, a second class passenger. An early filmmaker, his work helped contribute to the development of filmmaking during the early 20th century, and he may have been on board to record some of the maiden voyage for posterity. He had previously filmed the aftermath of the devastating 1906 San Francisco earthquake, making him was no stranger to chaos in the wake of disaster; however, this did not help him or his young mistress survive the sinking.

There were many families and children on board the Titanic as well. One such second class family was the Wells. Arthur Wells, the family's patriarch, had immigrated to Akron, Ohio two years prior to the sailing, and his wife, Addie, and two children, Joan and Ralph (both under five), were setting sail in order to join him. He must have been devastated to hear about the ship's sinking, but tremendously relieved that his family all survived: after struggling to reach the upper decks because of locked doors, they made it into the overcrowded lifeboat 14. Sadly, though, Joan had many health issues and died in her twenties. Her brother lived to be seventy.

Lastly, all members of the Titanic's band traveled as second class passengers. They were not technically White Star Line employees, but private contractors.The musicians, who were all English, included one pianist, Theodore Ronald Brailey; three cellists, Roger Marie Bricaux, Percy Cornelius Taylor, and John Wesley Woodward; a bassist, John Frederick Preston Clark; and three violinists, John Law Hume, Georges Alexandre Krins, and the bandmaster, Wallace Hartley. They were brought on deck near where the lifeboats were being loaded early on to help keep morale high. As the night went on and the situation became more dire, they continued to play, probably believing it was all they could do to express their own anguish and comfort the increasingly panicked crowd. Many survivors reported hearing them playing until shortly before the sinking.

There were more passengers traveling in third class than in first and second class combined. In fact, the White Star Line and other contemporary companies made more money from their tickets than they did first and second class passengers (not only were there more of them, they were much less expensive to take care of). While their accommodations were meager at best compared to first class, the Titanic's third class accommodations were advertised as superior to other ships making the trans-Atlantic voyage at the time. Many of the passengers were immigrants who planned to either stay in the United States permanently, or make money and eventually re-join their families back home. Proportionally, they suffered the highest casualties. Among these passengers, occupations ranged from laborer to servant or butler to scholar, farmer, jeweler, tailor, bartender, and housewife. Despite the call for "women and children first," many of these casualties were women and children. Twenty-seven year old Ida Livja Ilmakangas had traveled back to her home in Finland from the United States to pick up her twenty-five year old sister, Beata, and bring her back to the U.S. Both young women died in the sinking. Their bodies were never identified.

The Oreskovic family also traveled on board. Luka, Jelka, and Marija — Croatian immigrants in their twenties — all perished. The Joseph family, of Lebanese origin, was Detroit-bound on the Titanic. Like the Wells family, Mrs. Joseph and her two little children — Mary Anna and Michael — were on their way to join their father. While all three survived by boarding collapsible lifeboats, six-year-old Michael was separated from his mother and sister as they evacuated. It is difficult to imagine the panic his mother must have felt watching the grand ship slip beneath the sea, not knowing whether her son was on board or not, and her tremendous relief at being reunited with him on the Carpathia.

Sadly, not all families with children made it off the ship. The story of the Rice family is particularly poignant. Mrs. Margaret Rice was born in Ireland, and after marrying, immigrated with her husband to Canada and later Washington State. While in North America, she lost her first child as well as her husband in separate, tragic accidents. After her husband's death, she returned to Ireland with her five sons, but decided to move back to the United States and booked passage on the Titanic. She and all of her children, ranging in age from two to ten, died, and none of their bodies were recovered. Another survivor reported seeing her clinging to all of them, trying to comfort them, as she herself accepted the tragic end her family faced.

Finally, in addition to first, second, and third class passengers, the Titanic also had almost nine hundred crew members on board. While cruise ship staff today usually sign long-term contracts and stay on board the same ship for several journeys, this was not the case in the early twentieth century. Aside from the ranking officers, the majority of crew members were recruited in the weeks leading up to departure. Thus, many of them were from England, specifically the Southampton area. Only a handful of these recruits would be called "sailors" by any stretch of the imagination; the vast majority held a variety of other jobs. The engine required over 300 workers, while most others were employed as cooks, waiters, janitors and cleaners, maids, laundry workers, and a variety of other titles.

Of the ranking officers, most were members of the Royal Naval Reserve. The organization works much like army reserves: they are trained and could be called up in a time of war to serve their country. Captain Edward Smith spent most of his career working for the White Star Line and had commanded some of its largest, most important ships. In fact, less than a year before being given command of the Titanic, he was at the helm of the Olympic when it collided with a warship, but because of his long tenure with the company, the White Star Line never doubted Smith's abilities. He was not on the bridge when the new ship struck the iceberg that would doom it, but nonetheless, he attempted to manage the evacuation of the ship and died on board. His body was never recovered.

The second in command on board the ship was known as the Chief Mate. On the Titanic, this was Henry Tingle Wilde. William Murdoch was First Officer, and it was he who manned the bridge when the ship collided with the iceberg. Rumors abound that he committed suicide by gunshot in the minutes before the sinking, but there was always dispute among survivors about whether or not this was true. The Second Officer was Charles Lightoller, who survived the disaster despite staying on board until the ship was submerged; he found his way to a lifeboat and clung to it until he was rescued. Later, he served in both World War I and World War II. The Third Officer, Herbert Pitman, also survived, and he was the only one of the ranking officers who was not a member of the Royal Naval Reserve. He was placed in charge of rowing lifeboat 5 to safety, away from the ship, though he did not believe at the time that the Titanic was really sinking. After she submerged, however, he tried to convince the other members of the boat to row back to the site and save those stranded in the water, but out of fear of being overtaken by too many desperate swimmers, his command was overruled.

Chapter Five

The Iceberg and the Sinking

After the Titanic steamed out from Queenstown, the days of April 11, 12, 13, and 14 progressed normally. The Titanic made good time, traveling near top speed. The crew had few mishaps and did their jobs diligently, and the passengers of all classes enjoyed the various amenities available to them. The passengers and crew detailed above were only a few of the more than two thousand souls who would endure the tragedy on the night of April 14-15.

Perhaps you have heard the expression, "the tip of the iceberg." This means that while icebergs do not always look formidable above the water, what you are seeing is only the tip; they are much larger underneath the water and pose a serious threat to oncoming vessels, and it would be the under-water portion of the iceberg that would rip into the Titanic. It is well known that the Titanic received several ice warnings from ships steaming ahead of her during the voyage. In fact, seven separate warnings were received on April 14. The warnings about the dangerous ice reached the captain and other ranking officers from the Marconi telegraph operators on board. While it is easy to assume that folly or pride led these warnings to be ignored, that is probably not the case. As was stated previously, it was standard practice for the ship to continue on at fast speed even through ice-infested waters. Collisions of large ships with icebergs over the preceding decades had not resulted in disaster, and most ships depended on their reliable lookouts in the crow's nest to warn them about ice in their path.

The lookouts on the night of April 14 were Frederick Fleet and Reginald Robinson Lee, and they, along with the other lookouts on board, had all been informed about the danger of ice on the journey. Fleet and Lee were nearing the end of their two-hour shift at around 11:40 pm when Fleet spotted the iceberg that would fell the mighty ship. He followed protocol, immediately issuing a warning and phoning the bridge, where he warned First Officer Murdoch, as the captain had gone to bed for the night. Murdoch ordered the engines reversed and the ship to turn, hoping to avoid the berg completely. But his decision proved fatal, and the starboard (right) side of the ship scraped alongside the jagged ice underneath the water, ripping holes in five of the watertight compartments toward the bow of the ship. The impact was felt according to class: the crew members working in the bowels of the ship knew immediately that something was terribly wrong, and water reached them first. Third class passengers, especially those on the starboard side, were startled as they were awakened by the violent jolting, and some may have even heard the scraping of metal. Second class passengers felt a disturbance, but heavy sleepers likely slept right through it. First class passengers who were awake and attentive felt something, but probably attributed it to the sea. In fact, Fleet and Lee, who were at the highest point on the ship in the crow's nest, were elated, thinking that they had averted disaster.

Fleet and Lee would survive the sinking (they were ordered to man lifeboats), and both would testify at the inquiries held by the governments of the U.S. and Britain. Since Fleet spotted the iceberg, his testimony was of special interest. He claimed that, had he had binoculars, he would have seen the iceberg sooner, perhaps leaving the ship enough time to turn. The binoculars were a sticking point in the inquiries: neither investigation could confirm why the lookouts did not have them, though several plausible explanations were given. That said, experts generally agree that even with binoculars, the iceberg would have been very difficult to spot. It was an especially dark night, thus the lookouts relied mostly on light shed by the ship. It was also unusually calm, meaning that no water was breaking at the base of the iceberg, one of the best ways to spot one in the dark. It is in human nature to look for blame when such tragedies as the sinking of the Titanic occur, but the fact of the matter remains that the collision with the iceberg was likely not the fault of high speed, the captain not being on deck, ignoring warnings about ice, or the lookouts not having the equipment they needed or not paying attention. More than anything, it was probably due to profoundly bad luck.

Regardless, the next few minutes were crucial. In only about ten minutes, by 11:50 pm, water had risen fourteen feet in some damaged parts of the ship. No one among the "first responders" or high-ranking crew members doubted the severity of the emergency. Captain Smith was awoken at once and summoned to the bridge, and the watertight doors were closed. He and the ship's designer, Thomas Andrews, surveyed the damage below deck; by the time they did, the Titanic had already taken on a considerable amount of water and was leaning ominously forward. As the captain ordered the Marconi operators to begin sending distress signals and to summon another vessel, any vessel, in the area, Andrews told him that the ship likely had under two hours before it sank (in fact, the ship would not sink for almost three hours). Captain Smith was undoubtedly distraught as he ordered that the evacuation on the lifeboats begin at about 12:05 am. The Carpathia answered the Titanic's call for help by 12:25, but at their distance, they would not arrive until the ship was well under water. When Smith heard this news, he now knew that many people were likely going to die.

The ship's crew, and the ship herself, were ill-equipped to handle the sinking. Neither the White Star Line nor Harland and Wolff ever declared the ship to be unsinkable. Nonetheless, with technology like the watertight compartments, as well as modern shipbuilding in general, that was the assumption of the day, not only about the Titanic but also about other, similarly modern ships. As previously stated and well-known, the ship did not contain enough lifeboats for all the passengers aboard. The ship was equipped with lifeboats in the first place primarily to facilitate movement of passengers from one ship to another in the event of an emergency, not to evacuate and hold all souls on board. Yet even before the loading of the lifeboats began, the disaster was ill-managed by an under-informed crew. Perhaps in order to avoid panic, many members of the crew charged with interacting with passengers were not given full information. While their relaxed attitudes allowed guests to remain relaxed, it also gave the impression that perhaps there was nothing to fear; perhaps the captain was being overly cautious; maybe this was just a drill.

Other factors delaying the evacuation were the time of night and the weather. It was past midnight, and many passengers had retired for the evening. Those who were still awake were more than likely enjoying post-dinner libations, and thus their sense of judgement was impaired. Especially among the upper classes, ladies hesitated to leave their cabins without dressing at least a little, a process that took several minutes at minimum. Finally, the cold was a major factor — as stated previously, initially no one wanted to leave the warmth of the interior of the ship to sit in a boat, out on the dark ocean, in the freezing cold. Without a sense of urgency, who could blame them?

Ironically, the third class passengers would be last to reach the lifeboats but first to realize the severity of the situation. The ship herself was not only ill-equipped for such a disaster, but the crew was ill-trained (if trained at all) to handle a mass evacuation. Several staircases and doors remained locked, a measure taken to prevent third class passengers from sneaking into first or second class, but which ended up trapping people below decks, unable to reach the boats. While probably few people drowned because they were trapped behind locked doors, the delay cost many their lives, as half-full lifeboats were lowered onto the sea below. In fact, the first lifeboat, which could have safely held sixty-five people, contained only twenty-eight. Another lifeboat would only contain twelve people.

As the first lifeboat was lowered into the water, the first of eight distress rockets was also fired, in case any ship was in sight. Tragically, another ship was in sight, and did see the distress signals. The S.S. California was much closer than the Carpathia, and feasibly could have made it to the Titanic in time to save most, if not all, of her passengers. However, the captain of the California misinterpreted the rockets (sometimes ships fired them to let other ships know who was in the vicinity), and instead of summoning his telegraph operator, he had the crew use Morse code over lanterns. The Titanic was either too far away to see them (most likely), or too distracted. Regardless, the California did not learn of the Titanic's fate until the next morning, when it was much too late.

For those on board who knew what the rockets were for, they began to realize that the situation was serious. As the night progressed, the gravity of the situation became undeniable for more people, until everyone knew. The ship was tilting more and more toward the bow, and people were making their way from the lower decks, having seen the rushing water. As many survivors would report later on, chaos certainly ensued. There were also many heart-wrenching scenes. As noble as it sounds, "women and children first" was actually the law of the sea at the time, and many men were forced to say goodbye to wives or children, knowing or at least suspecting that they would not survive. At the same time, as hundreds of people flooded into space on the upper decks meant for leisurely strolls, the crowd separated families and friends, some who would reunite on the Carpathia, but many who would never see each other again.

The last lifeboat was lowered around 2:05 am. By this point, it was apparent to everyone that the ship was sinking fast. However, it is important to remember that not everyone still on board had the same perception of events. The ship was large, so not everyone realized that it was the last lifeboat, and many probably did not know that there were not enough lifeboats for everyone (although knowledge of that fact did spread). What is more, many people likely did not realize how fast the ship was sinking, or that the rescue ship was so far away. But while many doomed passengers may have still held out some hope (after all, it is in our nature as humans to do so), panic no doubt had set in for most. The people who had the clearest picture of what was happening were the luckiest: they were the ones in the lifeboats, who had rowed a safe distance away from the ship, and thus had a full view as the bow lowered further and further until it was submerged. It was necessary to row far away from the ship itself, as when the Titanic did sink, the massive size created something akin to a whirlpool, pulling anything nearby down with it. In fact, many people were pulled down with the ship, but eventually floated to the surface thanks to their lifejackets. Many of the people seated in the lifeboats had family or friends on board, and had to watch helplessly as the situation became increasingly dire. It was certainly a traumatic experience for everyone.

Even though the only ship that had responded in the area was the Carpathia, still a considerable distance away, the telegraph operators continued to send distress signals. The last one was sent at 2:17 am, when the operators were relieved from duty and the captain announced that it was every man (and, sadly, woman and child) for themselves. By this point, the bow was completely submerged and the stern was sticking up nearly perpendicular in the water. People were falling to their deaths against the mighty propellers or the frigid seas. At 2:20 am, the people in the lifeboats watched in horror as the bow, under strain, broke apart from the stern and went under the water. When it broke, the noise must have been terrifying for those on board, not knowing what was going on. Then, as the stern settled back onto the water, cries of relief went out. People still on board thought that the ship had corrected herself because she had settled back normally on the water. However, that relief and hope was short-lived: the stern rapidly filled with water and turned upright again before following the bow under the water. It remains unclear whether the bow and stern completely separated from each other before or after the ship was submerged. It is possible that the two halves broke apart completely as they sank.

As the ship disappeared beneath the water, its force pulled down people and objects in its vicinity. But minute by minute, people fought their way to the surface, screaming and crying for help. People in the lifeboats remembered the haunting cries, which began as a cacophony, and gradually grew quieter and quieter, until no one was left crying out anymore.

While it surely felt like an eternity for those who could hear them (not to mention those doing the screaming), most people did not last long in the frigid water. In fact, many people did not make it to the surface at all, especially as swimming would have been very difficult if they were not wearing a life vest or if they were inside the ship. What is more, once the ship submerged, full panic probably set in for a number of passengers. One of the causes of this — even when under water — is hyperventilation. Passengers would have inhaled sea water and drowned quickly. For those who did make it to the surface, the beginning effects of hypothermia would have set in rapidly, probably within twenty minutes at most. As the body works very hard to keep itself warm, it diverts blood away from extremities to its core to do so and to prevent more heat from escaping through blood vessels. Thus, without adequate blood to the brain, arms, and legs, dizziness or confusion soon develops, as does muscle weakness, numbness, and slurred speech. Body temperatures would have been dropping rapidly, as would blood pressure. With normal human body temperature 98.6 degrees Fahrenheit, temperatures of 90-95 degrees are considered dangerous, while temperatures below 85 degrees are fatal if not brought back up quickly. Eventually, due to lack of resources, the victims in the water would have slipped into comas and gone into cardiac arrest.

While so many people floated on the sea, dying, most of the lifeboats did not sit idly by. They had to confront the excruciating moral question of whether to put their own lives at risk and row back to pick up survivors, or whether to preserve their safety at a distance, and either hope that a ship would arrive soon (doubtful, since none appeared to be on the horizon), or let the others die. Most opted for the latter. Famously, Margaret Brown (discussed above) forced her boat to return, but by the time she had taken charge, they were only able to pull a few people from the icy water. The rest had already perished.

Meanwhile, the Carpathia was steaming toward the site of the wreckage. A telegraph operator had awoken Captain Arthur Henry Rostron when he received the distress signal. Rostron, was also a member of the Royal Naval Reserve, immediately ordered a reply and turned his vessel in the Titanic's direction. The Carpathia was a ship of the Cunard line, which he was sailing from New York back to Europe. However, in such a disaster, with lives at stake, it would not have mattered to any captain what company they worked for; the code that governed seafarers dictated that distress signals always be answered. What is more, Rostron was a devout Christian, and believed it was his God-given duty to help those in peril. He guided his ship as quickly as possible, but was delayed somewhat by dodging icebergs along his path. As they neared, they fired rockets to give hope to the stranded passengers, which were first spotted at 3:30 am. They began picking up lifeboats at 4:10 am. The process took several hours, and in all, 705 people were saved of the 2,223 on board. Because he did not have adequate resources to make it all the way to Europe, Captain Rostron turned around and headed back to New York. The Carpathia arrived three days later on the morning of April 18.

Chapter Six

The Aftermath

The sinking of the Titanic made front-page news around the world, and it was not only the death toll that was shocking. As previously stated, no one from the White Star Line or Harland and Wolff ever claimed that the ship was unsinkable. More realistically, the public believed it, because they had faith that human progress and innovation had overcome the hazards and obstacles of the past. They believed that all modern ships were unsinkable, and this event helped to shatter that faith.

The public in the United States, England, Europe, and the rest of the world was anxious for news of the sinking and word from survivors. A crowd of about 40,000 gathered on the docks in New York as the Carpathia arrived, and among them were many reporters. Also among them were aid workers and charitable organizations, there to help especially the immigrants disembarking after the traumatic event. Some survivors shied away from the press (notably, Mrs. Astor stayed somewhat out of the spotlight), while others became involved. As was already mentioned, Margaret Brown used the notoriety she got from her involvement in the event to bring attention to her numerous causes. Two of those causes became the reform of sea-going to make it safer and honoring the valiant of the Titanic disaster. She would be the one to personally hand Captain Rostron of the Carpathia the Congressional Gold Medal for his role in the rescue. It took several days for the complete lists of survivors and casualties to be released, as well. The anguish of waiting was felt especially poignantly in Southampton, as vast numbers of the crew hailed from that port city, and many died in the sinking.

There was an effort to retrieve some of the bodies left behind. The White Star Line sent several ships out to collect and bring back the dead that they could find. The first ship to reach the site of the wreckage was quickly overwhelmed. They preserved the bodies of first class passengers first, justifying their decision by claiming that these would be most likely to have property disputes ensuing from their deaths, and confirmation of death was needed. They wound up burying many crew members and third class passengers at sea. The other ships picked up dozens more bodies, and the last body was retrieved in late May. By then, officials concluded, life vests would have begun to disintegrate, and remaining corpses would have disappeared beneath the waves. In total, only about 300 bodies of the more than 1,500 dead were recovered. Some families traveled to Canada to claim their loved ones, while others were buried in the city of Halifax, Nova Scotia. There are still several anonymous graves.

Several boards of inquiry were convened in the aftermath of the sinking. The United States Senate (April-May, 1912) and the British Board of Trade (May-July, 1912) were the most well-known and well-publicized. Many members of the public followed these events as they unfolded closely. Both investigations, and all others conducted formally or informally such as in the media, clamored for an explanation. They all wanted to believe that they could find the reason, the explanation for the disaster. In other words, the public and the officials wanted to believe that there was a "smoking gun" that would explain the entire tragedy. However, they could not.

As have all been discussed above, blame could not be placed on the speed at which the Titanic traveled (most ships her size and age traveled at or near top speed). Nor was it because of the time of year (many other ships traversed the ocean during colder months). Nor was it because the ice warnings were ignored (they were delivered and the ship followed standard practice). It was not because Fleet and Lee did not have binoculars, or because the captain was not on the bridge. It was also not poor construction, or anything of that nature. The only explanation that could not be ruled out was that the disaster was either a complete accident: a series of follies that together resulted in horror, or simply an act of God. To this day, this fact has been difficult for many to accept, as legends, myths, and superstitions abound.

The Titanic passengers did not die in vain. As a result of the tremendous loss of life, international regulations were passed regarding lifeboats, telegraphs and communication, and ice. All ships would be required to carry enough lifeboats, crew would be trained to use them and evacuate, and passengers would have a drill so that they knew where to go and when in the event of a disaster (which anyone who has taken a cruise is well aware). Also, it was mandated that telegraph machines and later, other forms of communication, be manned 24-hours a day (had someone been at the telegraph machine on the California, they would have confirmed the emergency). Finally, patrols were set up to better survey ice fields and warn vessels about dangerous areas.

Conclusion

For decades after the sinking, the desire to find the ship never died out, as numerous monuments and memorials were built in sites around the Atlantic. However, even finding a ship at such a depth (about 12,000 feet below the surface) was a formidable obstacle. It was not until the 1980s that technology to withstand the amount of water pressure that deep was available. Then, in 1985, more than seventy years since it had sunk, an explorer named Robert Ballard located and photographed the site of the wreckage. Part of the reason that it was so hard to find was that it was several miles away from where it was thought to have gone down. What he, and others on subsequent visits, have discovered is truly remarkable. The ship retains much of its original structure, meaning that she has not disintegrated or collapsed. In addition, many artifacts have been discovered in the miles surrounding the wreckage: everything from toys to furniture to dishes to personal items (the remains of anyone on board would have been consumed by sea life and bacteria long ago). Talk about raising the ship has also circulated. However, such an undertaking may not be possible: first of all, while vessels can reach such depths, the kind of equipment needed to lift such a heavy load probably cannot (not to mention the power needed to supply it). Secondly, the ship is undoubtedly in fragile condition, and attempting to move it in any way may destroy it. Finally, many people view the undersea wreckage as a kind of gravesite or memorial to the people who lost their lives. Moving it would be akin to digging up the bodies. The wreckage is actually protected by United Nations law, much as other historical sites are similarly protected.

The Titanic continues to loom large in collective memory. Numerous books, television serials, documentaries, and movies have been made that commemorate or recreate the disaster. Most notably, James Cameron's 1997 film, Titanic, set box office records that took years to break. A permanent exhibit is installed in one of the most popular casinos on the Las Vegas strip, and traveling exhibits that feature artifacts recovered from the wreck site and donated by survivors also draw large crowds. Whether people continue to be fascinated with the tragic loss of life, the symbolic end of an era, the myths and legends that surround the sinking, or something else, there is something about the Titanic that has clearly resonated with people through its one hundred year history; it is realistic to assume that her story will continue to stand the test of time.

22620720R00029

Printed in Poland
by Amazon Fulfillment
Poland Sp. z o.o., Wrocław